THAW

poems by

Clarke Owens

Finishing Line Press
Georgetown, Kentucky

THAW

ACKNOWLEDGMENTS

The poems in this book were first published in the following journals:

"Thaw" in *Plainsongs*
"A Bullfight" in *Bryant Literary Review*
"Ovidian" in *Pinyon*
"Coast" in *The Inflectionist Review*
"Geotropism" in *Poem*
"The Death of Animals" in *Oyez Review*
"Apostrophe to Toilet Paper" in *Coe Review*
"Live Bait" in *White Pelican Review*
"Mature Taste" in *Amoskeag*
"Horse Burial," "Like Those Legs?" and "Dermatologist" in *Slant*
"Coming Out of Anesthesia" in *Karamu*
"Cat Burial" in *Convergence*
"Graphs" in *Freshwater*
"Auction" in *Penumbra*

Publisher: Leah Huete de Maines
Editor: Christen Kincaid
Cover Art: Clarke Owens
Author Photo: Clarke Owens
Cover Design: Elizabeth Maines McCleavy

Order online: www.finishinglinepress.com
also available on amazon.com

Author inquiries and mail orders:
Finishing Line Press
PO Box 1626
Georgetown, Kentucky 40324
USA

Table of Contents

Dedicated to Deborah

Thaw

When the snowpack bloomed
we dug tunnels, left footprints,
and now they're melting
as February's sun rekindles.

The thaw clears a patch on the roof.
We close our eyes so snow won't blind us.

Icicles weep, grieving for the dead
of winter. We hibernators
buried ourselves and woke up
coughing bumblebees.

The first chill breath
of spring shocks us awake.

Stop crying.

A Bullfight

Warily, the bull's hooves pound the sand—
black hide, muscle, churning with intelligence—
and he pees in fear. Lanced on his spine
like a triceratops, tortured by picadors—blood
black and shiny, streaming down his black hump—
the bull sees the sequined man turn his back,
toss his ponytail high, death-disdainful.
He lunges, upending the man, nuzzling a horn
lovingly into his leg. The man flips
like a doll, eyes in that moment empty
of drama, bravado: the universe has grown.
He's awakened from a dream, half-sick
and ashamed of trying to imagine an art
over which one has supreme control.

Ovidian

who were dancing
in the woods
    I became

        a bird
            ossified
      you became
        a stone
        flying

you flew
on your path
    I stayed
    where I was
        trying to remember

        the comfort of feathers

Coast

Driftwood bobbing on a wave, floating farther out
with each tidal stroke. It's like breathing.
Ocean has a cosmic breath, and someone ashore
is arranged like scenery, here for a moment,
like a deer crossing a road. Like forest
swallowing deer, ocean sweeps beach
in its seaweed-smelling compass, origin
of all that swims or walks, pebble
of the universe, and you to me like a sun
throwing off planets, are now cosmic debris
flying in mutually repellent directions,
crest picking up speed.

Geotropism

Detritus, mordant junk heap and decay,
what hopeless tropes to put you in your place?
What fangless barbs to mock your sad foray
of fluorocarbons and fracking apace?
It's you, great juggernaut, who will prevail
as poets cluck and hone their language tight,
rocking, rocking, rhythmic as we sail,
mariners of doom into toxic night.
As always, we can turn to trees and plants
to speak to us in green and silent ways,
and make our words resemble them, a stance
defiant, protesting our ending days,
and while our roots must cling to earth, devout,
seeing what's been done, like stems, we yearn out.

The Death of Animals

Picked off like Kewpie dolls in a shooting gallery
they go, the horse relieved of age,
the cat rendezvousing with the truck. I remember
an early girlfriend said, "Maybe
you're an animal," which, certainly,
yes I am. It's not only what's seen coming,
but what's here, the goneness of
their gentle, distinct natures, quirks
and fussiness too, the individuals.
Whoever has loved a Blue
has not sung in the heart the
dirge *Here, Old Blue?*
The cows of different colors and white faces
who visit the fence to cop a glimpse
of me with my tractor preclude my
ever eating a steak. My wife and I
have one parent between us, but there
were more tears for her mare than for
her mother, just as human calamities
somehow strike a harder place than
the homeless dogs of Katrina. "It's
because they don't understand," she
says, but for me it's simply the
inability to distinguish as I ought
between the kinds of beings we are.

Apostrophe to Toilet Paper

You come packaged
proudly as cookies
with your claims to preferment—
three-ply, baby-soft,
forest friendly—ferried
toward the scanner with bananas,
wine, dental floss. Even
your last name puts you
in the family privileged
with Shakespeare's art.

Alone, for relief,
all are grateful for you;
all pay close attention
to the signs they write
on your detachable panels;

and though frugal armies
urge your scanty use,
one wants your thorough services,
for you take upon yourself
a burden we don't wish to bear.

Yours is a sacred intimacy,
so far from degraded that only
loopy teenagers would think
to use you to bedevil neighbors,
bedecking evergreens in front of schools
but there you are,
long and naked testudo,
draping the raised arm
of the founder's statue
like the napkin of a maitre d',
your cylindrical origin

at his foot, a waste.

LIVE BAIT

She works in the carry-out near the state park,
the one that says "ICE" and "LIVE BAIT" on the side.

In tie-dye and cut-offs, she trolls the counter,
luring the owner from back rooms.

When no customers are near, he wades
                              behind her,
like the fish that swallowed Jonah.

A year later, she's dancing
in a sportsman's club, thinking
she should have quit that job
in that little town in hell.

She lifts a finger to a shoulder strap
and the salmon arc upstream.

Mature Taste

What enchanted directly still enchants—
snapdragon, swallowtail, sunset—
but some works were more nature, less art,
and now the eye discerns the gearshifts
of mystery, the tacked-up bungalows
behind the magic city, the banal
assumption behind the twinkling eye.
The novel once read with absorption
shows the seams and seals of its making;
the poem that mystified separates
into pliable flats and fliers.
The delight of our voyage shrinks
like the porch of our childhood
that rose to our thigh, and the stalks
of corn that pinioned the sky.

Horse Burial

How ignominious to be dragged with a line around the hoof
by a backhoe, to be pushed into the hole, head and penis
flopping. Your beautiful long legs reach up
as if daring someone to break them, scarcely covered over
when the dirt is replaced. There you'll lie, not you
but the great frame which housed you
and looked so noble on a hill, contoured with your fellow,
heads down, lips so nimbly tearing up the grass.
Goodbye, dear friend. Your lack of words
made you a more beautiful animal than us
who chatter foolishness our whole lives.
You were strong, yet tender, your cheek like silk,
your eye alert, taking everything in.
Your fellow calls out for you, and sensing you're gone,
stands silently, with a sense of injury,
no longer fully trusting us. He's alone now,
a herd animal without a herd, sensing
that life ends with something inconsolable,
that all the chatter of the people does no good.

Like Those Legs?

The sky is a deep underwater blue, going dark.
A mist is on the tree-lined hill, and thunder speaks.
Thunder says, *I have no patience with your thoughts.*

Three young women died this week,
victims of car accidents, the oldest eighteen.

My wife is out repairing the fence before darkness falls.

Events collapse, happen at once.

Meanwhile a man from the high school reunion
says he wasn't sure it really happened until
a friend confirmed it, but he remembers
a teacher lifting her skirt and asking,
"Like those legs?" And now I see

the dogs are running away—three dogs,
three directions. I'll never catch them.
They want to be free, to explore, off the leash.

I can't control anything.

Dermatologist

Moles, marks, fearsome small
anomalies that might be
cancer, blemishes— Doctor,
the depth of my beauty is in
your deft hands, if not
my incipient end. Discriminate
for me. Teach me what to fear
and what not. Dispel my shame
at loving my wrapper; share my love—
share my hatred of strangers
appearing on my land masses.
Let's go to war with them.
Even the benign little spots
caused by collars—kill them,
kill them all! Give me back
an image of myself untrodden
by so much time, and I'll leave here
proud to be untempted by brochures
on plastic surgery. *Not vain,*
I'll say, as I drive Route 3,
cotton taped to my face, smarting
from your deep discernment
of my blushing continents.

Coming Out of Anesthesia

You're expecting to go down the mountain.
Someone asks, "Are you cold?" You say,
"No," and the nurse brings a blanket.
Your legs begin shooting, trying
to dance the flamenco on the ceiling.
The dove is stirring as you seek
to alight. You ask for your teeth,
and they say your teeth are gone.
Then the dove is awake,
fluttering its white wings
in the dusty hovel of your body.

Cat Burial

She winds down, like the others,
loses appetite, begins the dull-eyed stagger.

Take her to the vet, the vet minces, "guarded."
You pay the last three hundred
but she comes home in a box,
a package of soft black and white fur,
limp, head wet from the treatments.

Find her a sack, dig the hole with a pick,
lay her in, find a good stone.
We'll abandon this place, leave behind
a little graveyard where careless strangers
tread the modest life we planted.

Graphs

Observe this graph.
It covers the last four million years.

We could be
ignorers of graphs
but there is something compelling
about those interlocking squares.
We want to crook our thumbs, fingers
into them like school fences.

Let's draw a graph of natural things--
plankton, frogs, honeybees.

Let's draw a graph of the poets
erasing themselves
with measured breath.

Auction

After the angels of death,
we come, like miners
shining helmet lamps
into underground veins.

A warehouse:
tables piled high
with glassware and dolls,
and hanging on a wall
a bright red guitar.

We haven't enough
to outbid the others.

Death has no guitar
for its angel.

The author is a lump of earth exuding language before going silent. You could take a handful of earth from the banks of the Sacramento River, and a handful from the banks of the Nile, and it would be the same earth.

Clarke Owens grew up in Sacramento, California, the son of an Anglo father and a Mexican-American mother, both schoolteachers. His first meaningful job was playing guitar for a pop/rock band in Los Angeles. He later became a typesetter in San Francisco, and wrote arts reviews for a tabloid newspaper. He held many other jobs, including teaching English at colleges and universities in Ohio and New Hampshire. In mid-life, he changed careers, becoming an attorney, and doing mostly criminal defense and appeals. He retired from this career after twenty years, and currently lives on a farmette in Ohio with his wife, poet, essayist, and novelist Deborah Fleming, and her horse and cats.

Clarke writes poems, stories, novels, and occasional criticism. He wrote mostly prose prior to the turn of the century. While practicing law, he would sometimes return to the university to teach the occasional class, which involved discussing poetry and fiction with students. After decades of doing this, he began to feel more confident about how poems worked. Beginning in 2006, he began publishing more poems in literary magazines. The poems in this chapbook are taken from those that were published from 2006 to 2017.